Trash Truck, Trash Truck, What Do You See?

Written and Illustrated by LeDarrion W Bonner

Second Edition with
Enhanced Illustrations
2025

Printed in the

United States of America.

For my son Kam,

Your curiosity, intelligence, wonder and innocent outlook on life continues to inspire me to be better! May you always find joy in the world around you, just like these busy trucks at work!

With Love, Dad

Trash Truck

Trash Truck

Trash Truck What do you see?

Recycle Truck

Recycle Truck What do you see?

Dump Truck

Dump Truck

What do you see?

I see a **black** street sweeper sweeping near me.

Street
Sweeper
Street
Sweeper
What do you see?

I see a purple diesel truck traveling near me.

Diesel Truck

Diesel Truck

What do you see?

Excavator

Excavator

What do
you see?

Bulldozer

Bulldozer

What do you see?

Fire Truck

Fire Truck

What do you see?

Ambulance

Ambulance

What do you see?

I see a pink school bus loading near me.

School Bus

School Bus

What do you see?

I see so many different and awesome children playing near me.

Children
Children
Children,
What do
you see?

A **green** trash truck cleaning,

A **white** recycle truck recycling,

A **brown** dump truck dumping,

A **black** street sweeper sweeping,

A **purple** diesel traveling,

A **yellow** excavator digging,

An **orange** bulldozer pushing,

A **red** fire truck spraying,

A **blue** ambulance helping,

And a **pink** school bus loading,

That's what we see!!!

"The End"

-About The Author-

LeDarrion W Bonner knows firsthand

that being different is a superpower. As a child

who faced reading challenges,

he transformed his struggles into strength,

building confidence and character along the way.

Today, he creates stories that celebrate

the uniqueness in all of us.

"Every challenge is
an opportunity to grow
stronger.

Every difference is a
chance to shine
brighter,
be great!"